I HAVE LOST THE ART OF DREAMING IT SO

poems by

Ace Boggess

Published by Unsolicited Press
www.unsolicitedpress.com

Copyright © 2018 Ace Boggess
All Rights Reserved.

No part of this book may be reproduced or transmitted in any form or by any means without written permission from the publisher or author.

For information, contact the publisher at
info@unsolicitedpress.com

Unsolicited Press Books are distributed to the trade by Ingram.
Printed in the United States of America.
ISBN: 978-1-947021-32-7

Again, for Grace

Contents

I. POETICS	1
"Are You Having Any Sleep Problems?"	3
"Do You Intend to Quit Smoking?"	4
"Do You Think the Guitars Are Happy?"	5
"Hello Dahling LOL Whatcha Doin?"	6
"How Do I Know When I've Suffered Enough?"	7
"Where Is Your Troubled Faith?"	8
"Do You Think You Need a Psychiatrist?"	9
"What Do You Often Lose?"	11
"Getting Ready to Enjoy the Apocalypse?"	12
"Why Do Bees Have Stripes?"	13
"Who Cares About Such Things When One Has Found One's Niche in Life?"	14
"So You Don't See How Very Comical Your Role Is?"	16
"Can You Hear Rain Over the Telephone?"	17
"How Did Your Father Spend His Spare Time?"	18
"So, What Happens Next?"	19
"How Can We Distinguish What We Know from What We Believe?"	20
"Why Are You Asking Me?"	21
"What About You Is Original?"	22
"Is Forgiveness Real?"	23
"What Happened to Just Playing Music?"	24
"When Will You Be Off Paper?"	25

II. ETHICS — 27

- "And Do You Also Believe That I Am So Very, Very Wicked?" — 29
- "Where Will the Turmoil End?" — 30
- "What If the Phone Rang, and a Voice Offered You the Past?" — 31
- "What Happens When You Break Down?" — 32
- "Why Hadn't They Yet Murdered Me?" — 33
- "Why Are There Days I'm Not the Person I Want to Be?" — 34
- "What's the Point of Robbery When Nothing Is Worth Stealing?" — 35
- "Do You Like Your Infamy?" — 36
- "...What Kind of Person Am I if in Encountering Others, I Love the Slimy?" — 37
- "Have You Spoken to the Enemy?" — 38
- "What Do You Wish You Could Dream?" — 39
- "What Do You Care About?" — 40
- "What Are the Issues That Matter to You?" — 41

III. METAPHYSICS — 43

- "What If There Weren't Any Stars?" — 45
- "Would You Ride a Rocket into Space?" — 46
- "Would You Like to Be on the Moon With Me, Darling, or Would You Be Afraid?" — 47
- "What Is the Most Heartbreaking Thing You Can Think of?" — 48
- "Why Is the Music So Haunting and Sad?" — 49
- "Is This the Noise You Hate?" — 50
- "Is It Too Late to Keep Your Secrets Safe?" — 51
- "If You Didn't Know Me, Would You Think This Was My Face?" — 52
- "How Does a Smart Phone Come to Life?" — 53
- "Would You Like to Meet Donna for Drinks?" — 54
- "Why Do We Need Robots?" — 55

"What Has Become of Freedom?"	56
"Should We Be Mindful of Dreams?"	57
"What's Your Favorite Way to Be Touched?"	58
"What Have You Shared?"	59
"Why Can't I Be Happy-Go-Lucky?"	60
"Just Ask the Count of Monte Cristo or Can You?"	61
"How Do You Mess Up Boiled Eggs?"	62
"And Indeed What Does the Price Matter, If the Trick Be Well Done?"	63
"What Will You Do If the Pain Subsides?"	64
"When Will I Be Happy?"	65
"Are You Setting Things on Fire?"	66
"Should I Be Animated?"	67
"Why Did You Smile?"	68
"What Feels Better Than Noise from Our Nights?"	69
"What Is to Follow the Night That Just Ended?"	70
Acknowledgments	73
About the Author	75

I.

POETICS

"Are You Having Any Sleep Problems?"

—healthcare questionnaire

I can't seem to finish my dreams.
They build to a sort of tension
too impassioning to stop—
little detective novels
I have written myself into.
As the clues add up,
as a spy watches me from shadows,
as I never see the monster
though I know it lurks, stalks,
I fail to find a climax
resolution. A door won't open.
Zombies pause for a smoke break
at 2 a.m., then quit their jobs &
won't return. I see people I know
having sex with other people I know
although I know they don't know
each other. They smile at me &
wave me on to the next room
as if there were an answer there—
filing cabinet filled with facts
I still haven't figured out by 6,
when I start reading *Exodus*
rather than *Revelations*, &
the Great Delete begins again
as I roll over to silence
the droning metronome
that urges me, *Get up. Now go &
play the song of forgetting.*

"Do You Intend to Quit Smoking?"

—healthcare questionnaire

I get up each day at six as I did
all those years in the penitentiary,
except that now I go outside,
feeling the chill of frosted grass.
Already in the dim last moonlight,
squirrels follow their trail of tears,
searching for a few lost nuts.
A chipmunk rides its bullet train
across the lawn & down some unseen
hole as if a pneumatic tube. I hear
but can't make out a biker gang of deer—
four or five from the sound of it—
stomping leaves on the other side
of the fence. Though my cough
might startle them, as, too, a menthol
scent of my first breath of morning,
they won't flee, their hearts
as at peace in a.m. bliss as mine.
These are what I must give up.
Why would anyone quit so much
to quit a thing so small as this?
To sacrifice the serendipitous,
O, lament. No choice ever
comes without its cost.

"Do You Think the Guitars Are Happy?"

—Cliff Isaacs

Tips lazing
against the fingerboard
as though a cheek,
as though the neck
of a wine bottle
curved flawless—
they feel this, take it in,
return a faithful moan.
Their mother-of-pearl inlays
flush & flicker in humid,
spot-lit afterglow.
How you caress the sinews,
how you smack the pick guard
with your thrumming nail—
their notions of pleasure
like a hand to your crotch
or lip to ear. If only
we could sigh our joys
from such simplicity,
breaths might quicken,
heartbeats jag to the rhythm
of a song. But, we are more
challenging instruments.
Our bodies twitter & crackle.
They shriek. We shy away
from all but saddest melodies:
our troubled notes,
our false, defiant chords.

"Hello Dahling LOL Whatcha Doin?"

—Andrea Fekete (by text message)

I'm tying my shoes much tighter
so my feet don't slip out & dance.
I'm gunning my lips with hot glue
to weigh the corners down.
See that shadow that looks like me?
Over there waving his arm in the air?
I'll slap the grin right off him.
Watch me. See if I won't.
There's too much of the frivolous
binding my arms with daisy chains.
I mean to put an end to it,
to burn down the candy house &
leave the witch. Call me bring-
down, killjoy, curmudgeon.
Try to spike my punch with sunshine.
No, Miss! I'm tired of all this
happiness—the birds
aflutter in my throat,
the steaks on the fire,
the cake in the pan.
Let me rest a moment
before the funeral of despair
begins with jazzy clarinets.
For whom they toll . . .
Oh, Lord, for whom they toll. . . .

"How Do I Know When I've Suffered Enough?"

—Jennifer Hall-Farley

Do not expect too much of your feet.
They itch, they tickle, they ache,
they strain to curl inside your boots
like pink armadillos protecting themselves
from the car that crushes them.

Forgive them their murderous rampage
through damp grass over acorn hats,
jagged bits of rock & glass,
bee stings inciting violence to your toes.

There is always one more indignity,
one last howl burning its brand in your heel.

Try not to feel sorrow for newer wounds.
They will have their days to languish
in their lavish scars. Today,

forgive each suicidal lunge
your littlest rapscallion takes
against a corner of the coffee table.
Allow your fearless ankle to dance

the Twist. When you think
you have suffered enough,
you will suffer more—
juking, jumping & walking away.

Your feet betray you. Let them
have their moments. Bathe them
in the trickle of a stream
scented with coppery oils.
Lead them, powdered & regal,
along the broken streets

to the guillotine.

"Where Is Your Troubled Faith?"

—roadside billboard

The queue at the tire shop waits for no man.
The mechanic works in strange & mysterious ways.
Dirty with sleep, my eyes straining against the light,
I must make this pilgrimage again.
So many malfunctions pile the cairn of a life, &
a man forgets none of them, though penitent
for ones he calls his own: pellet hole
through window glass, sapling snapped
by the bumper of his car, divorce
to the extent it belongs to him & is not
a flirtation between emptiness & hope.
Holy is the suffering. Holy are these moments
overcoming. *Hole!* is what the tire sings.
Swing low, sweet chariot, hymn to the death
rattle, soft words for the falling away.
Time to breathe in the stink of oil & grime,
time for peace. I go to the industrial church
where a choir of drills & chattering jacks
absolves me of all my sins but one.

"Do You Think You Need a Psychiatrist?"

—medical questionnaire

She will try to cure me of poetry.
She will set out to resolve my inability
to run when my demons enter,
knowing I would rather name them,
put them on display, ask them to dance
for guests & the neighbors peeking
through curtains for a better view.

I picture her sitting in shadows
behind a desk she wields like a granite wall,
her thumb & index finger stroking
the place where, if she were a man,
there would be a beard so flecked with gray
as to be stern but indecisive.

She will have blond hair, a shade
like gilded letters on a book's cover &
a face so plain & pretty I must
take note of it in my journal
while she takes note of my taking note

in hers. Where could this lead me?
When must the emptiness of easiness
stroke my forehead with its cooling palm,
urging, "Sleep now, it's okay,
it's time to sleep," while I shudder
from dread that lives in all confusion?

She will attempt to hypnotize me
with pocket watch, penknife's blade
of candle flame, or her soothing voice
directing "Go to your special place" &
won't succeed. I have nowhere.

I wander through the special places
of others. I swim in their cobalt seas.

I drown there sometimes & return,
hoping to see a glint of metal, shark's tooth,
nautilus, or whatever else I overlooked,
as hot sand burns the bottoms of my feet.

"What Do You Often Lose?"

—Facebook post

So many I forget their names,
the ones I've sought & missed,
those overlooked: gobs streaking,
spit across the sky, blurring
into absence of memory.
How many have I chased through clouds
like granite gates that never parted?
Through rain & glare of orange city glow?
One almost led to my arrest
for trespassing in a graveyard
in Ashland, Kentucky,
where darkness settled like a lover
over cool but dirty sheets.
Two at once I missed for months,
alone out smoking on a West Virginia hill,
cigarette's blade cutting its own gashes,
scent muted by pollen everywhere. &
everywhere was what I was after—
straining eyes, retraining them.
Even as a child I lost Halley's
ghost horse that beat me by a nose.
Why do my arrows slip their mark?
Why does the alien taunt me
from behind a blind edge
on higher ground? That awe
escapes me, & the joy of witness.
I stand alone in a universe of dust.

"Getting Ready to Enjoy the Apocalypse?"

—Ron Houchin, Facebook post

Before the streets run
wild with stinging vines,
before all jags
of broken glass
crumble
into fine silicate dust,
when screams
no longer echo
from revelers
dancing on the edge
of a precipice,
I shall wear
an orange suit
so that fire
recognizes
I'm a friend.

"Why Do Bees Have Stripes?"

—Jim Hayes

How they come out in orange afterglow past dawn,
mapping the world for forests of new growth:
blanket flowers like roulette wheels;
black-eyed Susans perfumed exhibitionists,
exposing their sex; lilies; cosmos; daisies.
How they hide to rest when twilight hums.

The encyclopedia swears
they wear their yellow as a shade of danger,
evolution's biohazard sign, &
black to mark the other boldest
while they hunt, their barely-legs bearing up balls of pollen
like suns dragged into place by the feet of broken gods.

I prefer art never to be rational,
as if instead the swarm mind delights
in painting warriors for war
or sending off acolytes decked in holy vestments,
to preach of a kingdom beyond the next garden
where light shines & bees go to die & be reborn.

"Who Cares About Such Things When One Has Found One's Niche in Life?"

—Louis de Bernières,
The War of Don Emmanuel's Nether Parts

I wonder, for example,
how different my course
if that girl in 1987
hadn't stood me up at the Whitesnake concert.

Were she there in the fifth row,
amidst the runoff from fog machines &
shrieking deafness of proximate speakers,
what new cities might have beckoned me, *Come?*

Imagine the two of us in our damp black tee shirts
as we stood on folding metal chairs,
her straight blond lines whipping back &
forth like a glittery weathervane.

We didn't refer to that music as *hair metal* yet,
but shared energy of bodies
stinking of sweat & spilled beer
was what our young brains
described as love. &

where would my bad marriage be?
Lost before it began, not after
so many years preserved
like a head in the cooler? Too,

there might be different jobs &
homes—the better & the not-
so-much. Or, maybe I'm wrong.
Maybe nothing would change
but the memory which,

frozen like a bug in amber,
at least would include her name &,

I tell myself sometimes,
the cherry-&-menthol flavor of her lips.

"So You Don't See How Very Comical Your Role Is?"

—Milan Kundera, *Slowness*

Even in the dream, we are not together—
together meaning 'a couple' but also
'prefabricated parts assembled with hex keys &
screws to form a functioning unit'—
though I walk freely through her new apartment
by the university, where she decided to take
classes (I don't know the subject,
assume it's anything but literature).
I can't speak, so let her do the talking:
old house too big, debts too high,
furnace too busy not working.

She finds no comfort in this world,
not the dream world but what world
this dream world reimagines.

I smell the city through her window:
grass & soot, oil & blood.
It would be so simple to get lost here,
to detach spirit from the skin it's dying in &
just move along, a spoke in the wheel.

She hasn't figured that out,
hasn't wanted it, though the strain
stains her eyes like too much drink.

I want to embrace her, want
to explain away these mysteries,
to promise hope & promise the new,
but promise only silence. I would leave
a trail of words through the forest,
but our bread has been devoured
with a glass of warm saltwater &,
here in a dream as in the real,
I offer nothing but my being there.

"Can You Hear Rain Over the Telephone?"

—Kawabata, *Thousand Cranes*

The slippery suction
from your new lover's footsteps

as he steps through a steam curtain
onto bathroom tiles—

all shine & magnificent sinews like Zeus—
into a colder hour. Nonsense,

of course. You're nowhere near the shower—
in the kitchen, I'm guessing

by the thudding strikes of fists
pleading their case against oven glass.

These are not happy times.
I ask you to sing me to sleep

but what comes out of your mouth
is the retching monotone of bullets

from a tommy gun—mean &
inaccurate. What should I say to you

when I prefer holding onto silence
like a ledge I stumbled over? &

you, when you recuse your voice,
quiet at last should come between us,

yet there it is: the sound of rain
on a window, on the roof

like an army marching to resolve.

"How Did Your Father Spend His Spare Time?"

—internet questionnaire

It was the 70s, & I too young to learn gamble.
Over a pool table's golden felt, my father
flung cards that slid like figure skaters
prancing to a perfect halt. His friends formed a circle,
telling jokes & smoking bland cigarettes
that smelled of the forest in a burning year.
I loved to watch them pitch the red,
white, & blue plastic chips into the middle.
Each disc, a piece of the twenty-dollar buy-in—
not a fortune even then—meant comradery,
gamesman- & one-upmanship, escape.
This was how I wanted to be like my father—
festive & playful, willing to risk—
for the few minutes he let me watch
before sending me off to a less mysterious room.

"So, What Happens Next?"

—Facebook post

I drive to Starbucks in search of lost people failing
well. There's the blonde—young, thin,
her forearms tattooed with bean pods & dragons—
crying at a corner table, both hands gripping her *grande* cup
as if it might erupt. Streaks of purple tears
swear her husband left her for another man,
or she mourns how low she's fallen,
having stolen trinkets from the Target store next door.

Then a young boy drops his frappuccino which explodes
like a paint can flung off a balcony.
I have witnessed the birth of tragedy when a single
pinkish droplet splashes less poetic brown suede of my shoe.

Soon, it's the boy's angry mother snarling through her shame face,
teeth like pencils grinding graphite down.

Not to be outdone, the barista in green
dances like Gene Kelly around a light pole
as he snatches up his mop & broom.
Long black hair makes night across the highways of his eyes.

I look around, knowing something's always going on &
something else will happen next. An ending,

never quite a resolution, I exit through the glass door, &
already I've forgotten characters,
misremembered dialogue for silence.
Even caramel spicing up my latte fades,
its flavor that of birthday cake
mixed with just a hint of burning oil.

"How Can We Distinguish What We Know from What We Believe?"

—John Van Kirk

when the candy-eyed clown tumbles down
a flight of stairs & doesn't rise again

when the Sacred Clowns of the Navajo speak
inside their masks

when laughter oh what have we?

when did it become so hard to say
goodbye image goodbye illusion
hello matter & understanding?

when I say God we loved his serious work
but not his comedies—
that should've been a clue

when I say it was Prof. Plum in the Conservatory
with a bottle of Jack

when one of us repeats the joke
still funny though we get it wrong

when we open the closet door &
find a broom where skeletons should be

when we dance if we dance
slipping past the darkness for a while

when we clap at the scene of an accident

when we walk away smiling

when we ask

when we know the answer &
never need to feel this way again

"Why Are You Asking Me?"

—Kirk Judd

You passed me a mason jar, moonshine-brimmed,
when we gathered with writers around a fire,
the many of us toasting the end of a festival day.
I was pushing my first book, & you were everywhere:
poet of mountains & dirt under the fingernails,
police sketch artist drafting West Virginia faces—
all the usual suspects. I don't remember the shine's taste
which says a lot about its qualities. I recall fire scent
like dust on an old TV & how I ended up in a cottage bed,
kissing the tight, tiny backs of two women,
each into the other, sharing the passion of their liquor light
with me. One's lips tasted of grapes & cigarettes,
the other's like cinnamon toast. Where are those
moonshine moments now? Where is the hospitality
of Cedar Lakes, the hills & hollows (*hollers*,
as we say)? I ask because you know
the stories: where swans glide across a mirror,
who lived & later died in the haunted cabin,
why our midnights furnish their own fog.
You've stepped from each rock to every other.
You've faltered. You have found your way.
Tell me, where among cicadas rasping might we
make our music, holiest with resounding hollow chords
(or is that also *holler* chords)? Where, to whom,
do I pass the jar? I ask because you tell it best,
staring the world in its eyes while I look down,
reading all the white space on a page.

"What About You Is Original?"

—Marged Dudek

It's not the sitting at a table's equator
writing poems by junk light,

not that ape-walk down an alley
to avoid the wrong crowd

or the right one. No,
it's not the punches I took to the face—

all men know what it's like
to be beaten down (it's like

falling off a high porch
with instant replay). Still,

there's something, some glimmer
of me-in-the-world that separates itself

from me-of-the-world:
I the feeder fish escaping

the maw of a whale,
I asleep among the poppies

dreaming adventure,
I the stage magician's greatest trick

before he died—a conjuring
for which there's no solution,

no logic path to pierce the illusion,
so even the I that's aware of me

can't find the wires
lifting me off the floor.

"Is Forgiveness Real?"

—Andrea Fekete

We forgive the winter snow its blinding
as we curse beneath our frozen breath.

We forgive traffic patterns,
small red cars moving in & out
at dangerous angles,
never think of these again.

We forgive ourselves the candy bar,
the dropped football in gym class,
the tricksters' lies
we tell about our lives.

We are holy men of minor trivia,
absolving a stubbed toe
as we ignore bones in the sack,
a cup of antifreeze left outside,
the second Iraq war.

What we fear we can't forgive,
we won't, so walk away.

"What Happened to Just Playing Music?"

—Andrea Fekete

I slept too long in the razor wire
where notes chimed like saw blades &
the moans welling from inside me
would eat away the lining of an ear.
I walked down the silent road,
through the silent fog &
the black & silent woods,
far from noisy afterglow
of a city we knew so long ago.
I left my guitar in the pawn shop.
I left my guitar on a bed of coals
as I hurried across, afraid
to slow-dance in the embers.
Were we not performers once?
Your hips swerved & trembled
to trilling rasps spent from your lips.
I shrieked like a seagull
calling to the sea. But,
music fades, & a song will end,
except in radio waves, I've heard,
which drift through space forever.

"When Will You Be Off Paper?"

—Jesse Counts

The cons refer to parole as "paper" &
work hard—the ones that do work hard—
to get themselves "off paper,"
to me such an awkward concept,
having spent my life trying
to be on paper, jotting notes
on earth scenes & the colors of the sky. Look,
there's my byline under *Felonies Committed*,
followed by not so much a verse
as a litany of ideas, then a lengthy bio. So,
now that my year is up &
there's a chance—just a chance,
just as justice is left to chance—
this paper life might unlock
its flimsy shackles. How wondrous &
stupefying must the future be? Yet,
not as scary as that first day on parole:
the walking through gates,
the driving away, not looking back
for reasons given in all myths
of the underworld. The cons
don't call that being "off stone,"
despite so many years
of cold granite floors,
likewise steel & razor wire.
They only speak of it,
when they speak of it at all,
as "out of here."

II.

ETHICS

"And Do You Also Believe That I Am So Very, Very Wicked?"

—Mary Shelley, *Frankenstein*

If I came to you with arms stretched wide,
bearing sugar-white & violet-leafed orchids,
you would see only the knife that is & isn't there.

These things stay with us: Cain mark, bloody A,
rap sheet like a litany or monument for the lost.

What has passed, though not between us, comes
between us. It lurks in subatomic memory,
all our electrons dreaming naked singularity—oh

to go back to neat & orderly nothing
from which something bloomed, an ever-
expanding splatter of dark energy & dark matter.

A man cannot undo the sudden burst of chaos
from which his life was ordered, though in the made
universe there's more than vacuum, radiation, &
the asteroid that killed the dinosaurs.

Romance, also: mooning, starry-eyed,
alive with comets that cross the clearest nights
when skin tingles from wind's verse &
you suddenly recall this morning's horoscope:

"Look past the horizon," it said. "The situation
could be volatile. Know what it takes to relax."

"Where Will the Turmoil End?"

—Mark Strand, "The Way It Is"

"They expect you to *self-report*,"
I recall one of the cons saying.
Consider how the language of parole
should be the language of poetry.
Gladly I would spend my life
on paper, self-reporting, self-
whatever. Instead, I must check in,
renounce the company of darkness,
say little & mean less, intent upon the silence
that keeps a man safe from himself.
When will the silence end?
When will paper wad itself up
to jump through a hoop of fire?
Not long, I trust. It's never far
between extremes: to find release
or reluctantly return behind walls,
the razor wire glinting
in sunlight like scythes.
So, this is my self-report. I am
neither good nor bad, right nor wrong,
a prisoner nor free. I swim
through gray spaces
like an unknown class of fish.
This morning, I witnessed a sunrise,
magnificent in layers of pastel
oranges & pink. I turned
my back for a moment, a breath, &
when I looked that way again,
it was gone.

"What If the Phone Rang, and a Voice Offered You the Past?"

—David Rigsbee, "Tedious Vigil"

I wait for the phone to chirp nervously
like a finch in cat wariness
so that I can say, *Hello, old friend*,
before discussing law, heartache,
the complicated rules of a hockey game,
whatever troubles him—this shadow,
the voice from a dream of hard sorrows,
belonging to a man I knew behind the wall.
He sent a message: *I have a question.*
Can I call? The pause since nags at me
like a nightshift guard demanding
we quiet the violence in our prayers.
What will be asked, what answered?
Why does a good man stain his palms?
I hope there's no body on the shoulder,
no shards of glass ensorcelling the floor
in the Department of Empty Shelves.
I hope, but know what's possible
for men like us who've tested the wound.
Part of me—the part that regrets,
the part that remembers—prefers
that my phone remain mute.
I wait as though by answering
I might absolve the terrible interim
of what sins I imagine when
I condescend as if a better man.

"What Happens When You Break Down?"

—medical questionnaire

My knees won't bend or straighten on the stairs,
so I might be trapped in this basement forever
or, just beyond the threshold of the complex,
unable to ascend to that paradise of my lover's apartment.
My hands stiffen from repetitive stress,
arthritis or fear of speaking through my pen. Hip,
too, fights a duel with lower back. Some days,
I feel as though carved from granite,
soldered to an iron post, or stomped by
a gang of bikers until my bones cry uncle &
won't forgive the skin that won't protect them.
I am not so old as the marriage of dust,
but older than coins in my pocket &
the taste of rain during a morning run.
How does it hurt so much to live? I ask
as I punch my chin, bash my teeth in,
kick my shins. At least I possess ten toes
to feed to a mower's blade, eyes
that have not yet stared down the sun
to see green circles & figure out
my enemy's enemy never was my friend.

"Why Hadn't They Yet Murdered Me?"

—Luigi Pirandello, *One, No One & One Hundred Thousand*

My sighs dissuade them: thick, buttery, full of sap
as though a voice that swears, *Oh, let them come!*
Resignation spits no stink of fear
spewing its sewage from the skin.
It's what they want: a certain satisfaction
from their games of life & death. But,
I neither weep nor scream.
Their daggers won't meet me half way.
Their noose finds no tree branch strong enough.
"Go on," I whisper. "Do your worst."
They shrug & fire their pistols in the air.

"Why Are There Days I'm Not the Person I Want to Be?"

—Daniel McTaggart

Days when a hot shower doesn't erase
those glue stains on an arm.

Days the answer is always *No*:
a soundless voice pleads *More &*
How about pizza? How about a gram of cocaine?

Days your walk by the river seems distant,
though still you hear disoriented seagulls
like swords being forged, &
the stories a woman told you once—
anti-nostalgic—about her childhood.

Days you wouldn't play guitar
even if the music opened a secret door in the dull universe.

Days when traffic patterns slow.

Days Facebook pages & iPhones
are blurry lights somewhere in the fog.

Days you'd skip entirely … but the noise!

Days you learn no answers.

Days you see on the TV news
a body found decomposing, torn & pasty,
in the Ohio & you convince yourself—
no matter what the anchorwoman says—
that it is yours.

"What's the Point of Robbery When Nothing Is Worth Stealing?"

—Alex Kendall

A lamp will catch scratch at a yard sale,
too that forgotten paperweight with portrait-
under-glass of a woman's silhouette.

Everything has value to a thief—
needy, adding up pennies to fix himself.
to pay off his debt to the shadows.

My stepbrother learned last month.
Importunate hicks from the hollow where he lives
cleaned him out, stripped his trailer,

took goods plus the urn with his father's ashes.
He said, "I bet they dumped him in a ditch somewhere.
Even if they're caught, I won't get him back."

His eyes tried to swallow back the grief,

cheeks restraining rage in a crimson straitjacket
as he thought about how a bucket
once full of powdered bones

might find the black market, blackest,
someplace a good man wouldn't walk
without at least a razor in his shoe.

"Do You Like Your Infamy?"

—Facebook meme

When a poet inscribes her book for me
with the message, "Stay out of trouble,"
a permanent admonition on the frontispiece of verse,
I know I have been memorable, my accomplishments
biting as fox urine, sold to scare off squirrels.

This was supposed to be about her, but in her gratitude
for my ten bucks, she has made the story mine
though I've entered a scene at the last,
wielding ax & wearing mask: the antithesis
of *deus ex machina*, bandit with a heart of coal.

Is this my role in the drama? Prisoner
unleashed on a sleepy, unsuspecting world?
Cowboy in the blackest hat, firing off his pistols

at the moon? See? I've come this far &
yet to praise a line she wrote, one in which
I smell ripe apples as I pluck words from a tree.

She has seen the Thou of me, dark
as airplane shadows or a slurry pond.

What have I given back? Ten bucks &
the promised friendship of a stranger,
stranger still in the prison of my past.

"...What Kind of Person Am I if in Encountering Others, I Love the Slimy?"

—Sartre, *Existentialism and Human Emotions*

When I spoke at the N.A. meeting,
I told the others I understood
the need to give up junk,
but didn't realize I also
had to give up junkie girls.
I love to receive the damaged
with a grin & want to say,
"Show me your scars"
as if a familiar greeting
between old war vets.
The blackness in their eyes & clothing
brings such color to my life
as they tell their stories
of broken childhoods &
bad marriages. How I value
the emotional complexity it takes
to be so emotionally detached.
They walk into my many lives
wearing chimeric faces.
They sit at my tables &
stare at my cups of coffee
as if seeing there the battlefields
they've walked. I want to
embrace them with words &
arms & stories of my own
that are about them.
Is it wrong of me
to covet the woman
who gets the weirdest tattoo
just so someone will ask her
what it means? "Come,"
I say to her. "Show me
your scars." & she does.
She does. She does.

"Have You Spoken to the Enemy?"

—overheard in a coffee shop

Stop counting how many fingers
you have left & forgive the absent eye.
Murder moves mountains in your heart.

You would be like him? Tormentor?
Chattering prosecutor slamming
cynical briefs on the hardwood desk?

Is it victory or vengeance that seals
your bloody lips against progress? Talk,
talk to the hangman before he slides the knot.

Ask after his children & describe a film you saw:
the one where forgiveness wins in the end &
all become lovers in a world of disintegrating colors.

Say "Good morning" once before missiles rise
from their anxious tubes. It's not too late,
never too late to reach a deal, open up debate, &

surround, at last, the armory with tulips.

"What Do You Wish You Could Dream?"

—Natasha Sajè

To hold warm air against my cheeks
like an embarrassed blush,
to touch the sunbaked petals of wild irises,
I escaped shackles that froze my feet,
the chilly stare of a camera's lens,
the house of meanness boarding only men.
These sleeps I savored with their many offers of release:
happiest the hours I lost walking
uphill away from dark-eyed armies
guarding me with their marksmen's sites.
Safe now in false mercy of the outside world,
I have lost the art of dreaming it so:
to ride those highways past electric fields
of orange & magenta, lemon & emerald,
scented like fine mist from a bottle
along roads I traveled once,
not wanting to open like a flower myself
where my pillow lay crushed against its iron bed.

"What Do You Care About?"

—political leaflet

always words—not these
tattooed on a page but those
I couldn't speak as I sat alone &
buried my face in gravel
on the playground
hoping no one noticed
hoping someone did
then in high school
winding the corridors
silent as if after a betrayal
my mouth was a glue trap
from which those hissing
monstrous spiders couldn't flee
later too in bars & coffee shops
at home under yellow lights
not even to my wife
or those I swore I loved
I left my voice
in a bottle corked
I threw it far into the empty sea

"What Are the Issues That Matter to You?"

—political leaflet

Grace sends pictures of her orchids
in their second bloom, not pink or violet
but the color of lips stained by cotton candy.
How long she fretted, flooding them,
fearing they'd die unnoticed on a windowsill.
I'm responding with a message
of praise & awe when my mother calls,
tells me her SUV overheated
forty miles from Fayetteville.
She doesn't need a ride, she says.
The tow truck driver will take her
where she's going. I sense a chasm
has opened underneath her feet.
I envision her falling as she speaks,
wait for her to rise again like orchids.
Two different images—I know
these are the things that matter:
what lives on, what crumbles,
what sings, & what's then rent
upon the rocks. Why do we want
a world without such complications?
Every orchid is a phoenix flower,
meant to fade then blaze from ash.
Cars will fail & be rebuilt, as we will.
Each next step's a mystery, &
sometimes, far from home, a busted hose.

III.

METAPHYSICS

"What If There Weren't Any Stars?"

—William Stafford, "What If We Were Alone?"

The astrologers find other jobs:
mining the veins of umber leaves
for information, predicting futures
by digging graves—the easiest answer.
Captains of ships, stranded
in an age before technology,
refuse to sail at night, directionless,
each a compass in a room full of magnets.
No philosopher muses on the Infinite.
No scientist measures the speed of light.
No father, lying back on a beat blue Dodge,
says, "Look, there's Orion's belt,
the big & little bears, & there,
that's the face I drew for your mother
so long ago when we still loved each other."

"Would You Ride a Rocket into Space?"

—internet survey

to paste my image on the blackdrop of the Infinite
to feel small smaller less than a speck
to evacuate the sensual heaven of smell & touch &
    give over to eyes their pleasure
to understand drift orbit zero-G
to be a fly in the soup with diving suit & shades
to say "my God" & mean it
to learn how anywhere can be the same as nowhere
to undergo treatment for feet-firmly-on-the-ground &
    also head-in-the-clouds
to want this
to want more than this & nothing more than this
to study the strange from alien vantage &
    even then
to see my house from here

"Would You Like to Be on the Moon With Me, Darling, or Would You Be Afraid?"

—Simone de Beauvoir in a letter to Nelson Algren

Or Mars. The group
plotting to send colonists
for the rest of their lives,
perhaps noticeably brief,
has noted its one hundred finalists.
Not us. It could be us:
the aliens on an alien world
staring up at a sky passion pink,
our hands toiling in the forge of jags
on that strange earth
that isn't Earth & isn't
where our hearts grow stagnant,
fat: we the meaningless,
we the rut-stuck, we the longing
for a place where love
might be the only thing that blossoms.
At least we would have
our nights together,
nights that half the Martian year
are twice as long.

"What Is the Most Heartbreaking Thing You Can Think of?"

—David Lehman, "Who She Was"

I go back to the rose petals in a storm's wake:
cross-sections cut from a lipstick tube, snack chips
made of bubblegum scattershot across the lawn.
Radiant, they shone between jade of the forest &
ash-cloud sky. Wind speckled them everywhere
as though flower girls in apricot dresses came this way,
preceding the bride, or following. Yes,
other storms haunt me: parents divorcing
when I was eight, a friend's overdose
I didn't hear about until I saw his face in the daily edition,
wailing voices for weeks on CNN after the towers fell, &
all other wailing voices all other times on CNN. But,
those petals: they should be hung from museum walls,
a display of the Artist's master work. It was my yard then,
attached to a home I shared with a wife I embraced,
approximating love, & I hurried to push the mower
before sun's heat or return of rain could halt my progress.
The grass had grown long & weary, hanging its many heads.
The mower whined as if in remorse as it cut across
those pinkish serifs, composting them into glitter &
dust, removing what was briefly lovely
in a world grown ugly as an oil-stain face
on the asphalt of a highway out of town.

"Why Is the Music So Haunting and Sad?"

—Gao Xingjian, Soul Mountain

The singer died a few years back,
unnoticed then. We still listen
to his screeching, morbid laughter
as he mourns a day when he will die,
we will, or the world.

The woman next to me
has stopped her medication
because familiar darkness found her.

I'm smoking more than ever as I drive,
sweating through my collar
how a priest must,
standing up front in his humid church.

Still, the songs remind me, &
songs don't remember what they said, &
songs make everything better
even when they don't, which is
more often now for her.

Me, I'm all ears, thinking,
Tell me something—
anything at all I want to hear.

"Is This the Noise You Hate?"

—overheard downtown

Babies with their demonic bullhorns
sound like alarm clocks on TV:
old-fashioned pot-banging clatter
or the digital chirp of a robot chick,
I put on headphones, move to another seat
before I realize I'm trapped by jackhammers
laughing from four corners of the city.
Rap bass bounces by like tires blowing flat.
A rescue chopper above rasps its menacing purr.
A woman near the ice cream shop
shouts *"Jerry! Jerry! Jerry!"*
as if channeling a British soldier
warning us all of the Nazi advance.
At least the book store has imprisoned quiet.
I go inside, consider heading for the coffee bar
to synthesize my own adventure:
caramel, or maybe crème de menthe.
I love how the barista works the knobs &
metal pitchers, even the steam
despite its heavy snoring. I love
how he says, "*Enjoy,*" in a whisper
as if there's a conspiracy between us,
as if a theft of quiet ours to keep.

"Is It Too Late to Keep Your Secrets Safe?"

—news tagline on CNN

I used to hold on to them like hundreds of pills
with side effects all forms of loneliness.
Secrets stink of empty rooms, dust on bookshelves,
dangling spiders petrified from grief & loss.
I won't go back into that rundown house,
its blinds pulled, its door safely double-locked.
I prefer standing bare-skinned on a stranger's lawn,
shouting, *Look at me! Look! I'm a fool!*
to know that even the ugliest truth soothes
like the cigarette after an argument.

"If You Didn't Know Me, Would You Think This Was My Face?"

—Rachel Hicks, Facebook post

We can't call this sideways glance a lasting impression.
We can't know anyone.
People we meet in bars along the grayed-
out avenues of Huntington
are ghosts hopping in & out of frame
at times no one's finger clicks the shutter button.
Did we see that? Did our eyes lie?
Even those to whom we feel closest
keep their secrets from us: lovers, hidden bank accounts,
the unvoiced urge to hunt big game in Africa
because they read Hemingway in school.
We won't believe the acts they do,
as they deny us our *us*ness, too.
Our faces, like theirs,
become vapors seen through azure glass—
transient, bending images—
until we're not what we witness either,
minor characters in stories we tell about our lives.
What do you wear beneath the gold party hat?
How do you embrace deception?
I once said violence
was the most authentic thing I ever did,
by which I meant I thought myself innocent
& was wrong.

"How Does a Smart Phone Come to Life?"

—internet ad

From my laptop, I send a Facebook message.
It's 6 a.m., & she writes back, "I should
turn off my phone. This woke me."
I forget how folks fill up their phones
with restaurant locaters, weather data,
family albums, pornography, sonnets
which are like sixteenth-century porn with a lisp.
I forget, so wake them with my notes saying nothing,
notes that could wait until noon.
It's not like I'm confessing my crimes
or typing a love letter, more like
in my eagerness urging "Tattoo fire
on your back so you never lose it."
It's the mechanics of misunderstanding.
A *deus ex machina* comes to save the day
but misses, rattles a window instead. But,
what if I were to type some truth &
send it across those a.m. circuits?
Would that set off her improvised alarm?
Would it chime in the bell tower?
Rumble like a coal train blocks away?
Or would this be the time we miss each other
like satellites squawking our code
through ambivalent space? Adrift,
we go on circling, circling, falling, &
the quietest word in the dark becomes a scream.

"Would You Like to Meet Donna for Drinks?"

—spam e-mail

Lord, oh must this be my want?
Lust for tipping my glass with a stranger
(stranger than me, at least)? I get it:
she's a figment underneath the firmament,
her numbers drawing curves in code.
I'll find no existential Donna,
no liquor-*in-itself* for me to toast her with.
Yet she calls to me, invisible & sad
as if lost in one of my labyrinthine dreams.
Please answer, she begs. *Come,
meet me. Fondle my image beneath
a shroud.* Be sure to bring your credit card.
Part of me wants to take her
for karaoke, to hear her sing "Fever"
while I swoon. How backlighting
halos the pixels of her crimson hair
against my glimmering plasma screen.
How her voice issues clean,
annunciated syllables as if I could
hear her, hold her mouth to my ear.
She'd swear she loved me
for my identity, only truth she gave
before we reset our bodies
in the Ctrl-Alt-Del of our modern lives.

"Why Do We Need Robots?"

> —overheard in a restaurant

When we hold them close, press them to our chests,
breathe in their heavy oils & burning dust off circuit boards,
their cold hands addressed to our blushing cheeks
like an iron mask or two coins having missed the eyes,
we are comforted by their great indifference,
affectless. When we sit across from them,
sipping lukewarm whiskey out of paper cups &
playing chess or Stratego, their skill at games
teaches us to be better than we are.
When we say, "Take out the trash,"
they carry sacks of garbage to the curb.
When we say, "Mow the lawn," they do.
Later, leaning together on the sofa,
watching a movie about love that fades,
they never interrupt with questions,
although they miss the point, as we did once
when bug-eyed beasts & lasers were enough,
when our passions had yet to break us—
mechanical men that we, ourselves, became.

"What Has Become of Freedom?"

—Bob Hicok, "To Find the New World"

The trouble with freedom is being free
not to think about freedom or desire escape
to freedom. Easy spending too many hours
watching the same news on television
with nothing new about it to make it news

except in name. The machine god pulls its levers &
an airplane disappears—sleight of a clockwork hand
as repetitions of uncertainty go on for weeks.

There's a shooting in Texas which, at least, is fresh.

We are drawn into these other lives & so we forget
to live. Without the icy chill of steel shackles
there as symbols, we no longer feel the bruises

on our wrists. We watch a film in which some comic-
book hero fights to keep us safe. We eat fine meals.
We work, doze, blot out the sun. Why did we
want so much to break our bonds for this?

The trouble with freedom is forgetfulness.

The trouble with freedom is *I don't know,*
I'm bored, you choose. We suffer no prison
like the one we build for ourselves—
its walls of sleep stacked from cinderblocks &

routine. Where did we put the gate?
We never look for it. There are games
to play, & lights-out comes too soon.

"Should We Be Mindful of Dreams?"

—Hermann Hesse, *The Glass Bead Game*

She tells me she tore her heart from her chest—
not the valentine, the paper pretty with its buttocks &
razor point, but the gruesome strawberry dripping
juice—& handed it to me: not the me in the mirror;
a panda that was also me, fat with devouring urge.
Her elephant god looked on, scowling, scorned
by the diversion of a tribute that belonged to him.
How easygoing so much strangeness seems at night, &
how apt the metaphors of the unconscious. I could be
that creature full of cuddle & brutality, whereas she
might gash herself apart in love or sacrifice.
Everywhere a maelstrom ravages the body's rest, &
the mind that never rests as it creates its gorgeous,
frightful anime. What if it were not a dream at all,
what if the butterfly saw itself Chuang Tzu?
Just yesterday, I watched a squirrel standing
on a tree branch, forepaws gripping a slice of pizza.
The triangle dangled like a dart pointed down,
while a furry mouth made meat of its crust.
This was no dream, though it had the same
character of fantasia & meaning, definition:
such consuming, such taking in of the sacred &
profane. No, I'm not saying to her give me your heart &
I will give you pizza. No, I don't know
what I'm saying, except give me whatever
you choose. I accept it, will not consume it,
will store it in a locked & lacquered box
cushioned within with silks of infinite colors.

"What's Your Favorite Way to Be Touched?"

—internet questionnaire

We sat cross-legged in the smoking room,
her artwork on the floor between us:
charcoal blurs simmering swirls
like night-terror visions of a schizophrenic.
She ran hands over the page's plane,
stroking, soothing, sensual.
Fine black powder gathered on her
fingertips like newsprint.
This was news: I saw an eye, shoulder,
raven swooping from behind.
As I watched her fairyland unfold,
she reached out, feathering my cheek,
smudging me with soot in streaks.
She offered me the tenderness
she gave to the texture of her canvas.

"What Have You Shared?"

—Jennifer Hall-Farley

Do you remember opening my mail?
How your nails pierced the seal,
pricked the fold, a peeling more tender
than with the foil wrapper on a chocolate bar.
I watched you unsheathe a page,
snatch-purse lifting my fortune from a cookie.
I felt as if we were having an affair,
waited while you read the note.
Your lips fluttered, mouthing yes.
"Acceptance," you said. "Is it always
that easy?" It wasn't. "Lucky,"
I said. "Send your message out &
suffer hope until the answer comes."

"Why Can't I Be Happy-Go-Lucky?"

—Andrea Fekete

because men leave you—their natural state is waning
from shadows in all corners of the room

because the Russians invaded Crimea
which sounds like the punchline to a joke that ends with "river"

because an airplane fell from the sky unnoticed by you
or anyone whose job it was to look

because your mother ... because your mother

because water grows fetid on the tongue

because seven heads & seven horns

because you sometimes play both sides against the middle

because you laugh & then forget
until laughter turns into regret

because Clinton Bush Obama wait why care? you care

because you wear a necklace made from bone

"Just Ask the Count of Monte Cristo or Can You?"

—AceBot on what-would-i-say.com

Dear Count, tell me about the wind at sea.
You wait it out. It stares you down
while creeping up behind. It pokes your ribs.
It laughs, but soon it goes away until you
pine like a star-struck teen for its return.
Monsieur Dantès, what insights regarding love?
That dirt-encrusted conch that puts
the lie of an ocean in your ear? Go slow,
slower. Survive a bonfire on the shore
to see what embers smolder,
what artifacts outlast such godless heat.
My friend, Edmond, oh, what of revenge?
That too steps its slow dance between wind &
flames, between a rocky cliff & biggest waves.
It requires so many disguises you forget
the look of your own face in the mirror, &
the hand you see drawing the blade
is not the one that returns it to its sheath.

"How Do You Mess Up Boiled Eggs?"

—Jeff Carter

Insult the hen before she's due.
Refer to her troubled past:
absent father, a few bad marriages &
next you know she's out pecking scratch
behind the shed. Worry her boldly
like a televangelist who sneers
at his aging congregation.
Ruffle her feathers, mock her empty nest.
Assure her her eggs won't amount to much,
all of them born bad, already half-
way to the wastebasket. Now,
gather the survivors, collect them
in your spite basket, cuss them
on their quick trip to the spa.
Where water rages, let it hiss & sing.
Now drop them in. No easing. No
testing with a toeless foot.
Drown them: a dozen Ophelias
in their white wedding dresses,
but as they sink, assure them
just how sorry you are
for what you've done &
what you have to do,
how this last thing will
hurt you more than them.

"And Indeed What Does the Price Matter, If the Trick Be Well Done?"

—Joseph Conrad, *Heart of Darkness*

It is that: a sham, the illusion of isolation done
with two-way mirrors in the interrogation room,
a riddle we rhyme for ourselves,
no answer we might give to spare us,
to keep our bones in these flimsy sacks.
The going-on compels us: the looking
out through prison glass of bad marriages,
humdrum reality shows & assignments
from the boss who disappears in a puff of smoke.
If you wrote your last love letter at eighteen,
does it mean you are unloved, unloving,
when you reach forty-eight? Why deke &
miss the shot? Why be the woman in the box
when you can be the saw tearing through life
with jagged teeth & whimsy? Step forward.
Be part of the trick, not tricked by it.
Soon, the cards wear thin. Soon,
the rabbit leaves your hat—heirloom
from a vanishing act, so nothing remains
but to wear it on your head.

"What Will You Do If the Pain Subsides?"

—medical pamphlet

If withering bones hollow out
like those of birds, will I take wing?
My joints—ankles, wrists,
knees—needing a squirt of WD40,
sing chattering hallelujahs when I move
as if Handel's *Messiah*
transposed for cricket & cicada.
What lies my sinuses tell my eyes,
squinting, indifferent to the ache inside.
When does growing older
transform into growing old?
When does the cough of a cold
etch scars in the throat
that never fade? I should
break my nose on a stranger's fist
to remind me, even at my age,
some things heal.

"When Will I Be Happy?"

—Andrea Fekete

It's never too late to learn to play the piano,
to sit square-backed on a bench
before that coffin
in which the remains of so many masters
are interred.
You might hear
what Beethoven heard in his mind,
earless as a dog mauled for fighting speed;
or Mozart's intelligent frivolity,
leaning desperate, then syphilitic,
growing mad. How you might
feather the ivories like a lover's back
or a swath of silk,
how you slam them down
to push your rage into them
like the coin slot in a glass pig.
You've put aside passion
too long, longer
than this need for noise
in your quiet life allows.
Take up the melody.
Find what music's in you,
find the pedal for sustain—
now hold it there
until even the echo of doubt
chimes lovingly &
lovely in the air.

"Are You Setting Things on Fire?"

—bartender Eden Hodges (2002)

Watching the burn: paper scrap in an ashtray,
fragment torn from a cocktail napkin—
it flares center out, circle expanding,
a festive sunburst balloon.
One lover's cryptic message to the other,
it vanishes to corners, hints of passion
or remorse. It's halfway lost
before I perceive a worn line
I jot on back of my hand for later:
My fingertips remember best & miss you most.
Then, as I push this kiln across the bar,
how it fills itself black with ashes,
slides away like a dancer whose
body evades a spotlight in the dark.

"Should I Be Animated?"

—FAQs in an e-mail from Quiddity

Draw me—bulging-eyed
in Loon lust for that
mad jack in drag.
I don't care. I'll catch
the mouse, eat the sardonic
custard-blob canary.
Lip smack. Got it. Gone.
No fooling around for me.
No attempt to walk on water,
air, railroad tracks that
run through a cave wall.
My gadgets work:
I buy at Walmart
not three for a dollar
on Acme's home
shopping channel. So,
go ahead. Draw me
furry & naked with hunger.
Round off my claws.
Scratch behind my ear
with your pencil. This
is what I've wanted:
a little revenge for years
watching the rat-led rout.
Give me bomb & rocket pack.
Give me a butterfly
net & a hammer. See,
the meek might inherit
the Earth, but not
this one. Hang a sign.

"Why Did You Smile?"

—Charlotte San Juan

Half-hearted, the promised snow
finger-flicks against my cheek.
Baptized in dark, I lean
into a drag from one of those cigarettes
I know I should quit but love
now that my other habits have been lost:
narcotic haze of junk light blurring time;
liquor lens like detergent,
making brights brighter & bleaks bleaker;
lips like magnets, pulling mine.
For now, the rain/snow cleanses
like a rag against my face.
I hear deer in the woods: blackened invisible,
they romp through mounds of leaves.
Above, the sliver of moon
like a pinky ring for the Divine
has blinked out of bling behind clouds.
I look for it as icy droplets
run along my skin: tears
on a granite monument.
I catch them in my mouth,
that beggar's bowl.

"What Feels Better Than Noise from Our Nights?"

—a line found in an old notebook

How the first guitar chord—
key of G, merry, vibrant—
thrummed from a speaker,
riding over skin already in
the dope metamorphosis.
My friends & I felt it:
rhythm bopping our heads
like those of pigeons,
patterns of fingered runs like jazz
with blur & contempt,
tone of a singer seducing
as if from across
stray ridges of blankets.
We raised an empty glass in toast.
We tapped the tops of salt shakers
utilizing our coffee spoons.
We sang along as if we knew
words, their meanings,
as if we could penetrate
complexities, how hum &
screech will merge.

"What Is to Follow the Night That Just Ended?"

—Milan Kundera, *Slowness*

I awoke free as the jawbone of a spaniel—
bouncing, demanding, receiving—free

from the prison & free
from invisible bars that held my name to a page.

Gone are the parole office,
its overhang of unease

that this day might latch new shackles to my wrists.
I am free to look out my window, see ice on the walks,

free to walk them anyway
filled with dizziness & uncertainty more common.

Some days, nothing changes:
the eastern horizon smokes its pipe at dawn;

the government plods along,
embarrassed by its own weight;

the rover on Mars says, "Dust," &
to dust it shall return.

This day is not one of those: I awoke
with a key in the crook of my arm,

a jackhammer cradled against my neck.
As I take my first hesitant steps

from bed, even that hesitation
excuses itself, bows & moves away.

This will be a day of rioting,
reversing the old clichés:

at last, I am innocent again.

Acknowledgments

The author wishes to thank the following publications in which these poems first appeared, sometimes in slightly different forms:

The Alexandria Quarterly: "Why Do Bees Have Stripes?"
American Literary Review: "Are You Having Any Sleep Problems?" and "Do You Intend to Quit Smoking?"
The Asheville Poetry Review: "Why Hadn't They Yet Murdered Me?"
burntdistrict: "When Will I Be Happy?"
Carbon Culture Review: "How Does a Smart Phone Come to Life?" and "Why Do We Need Robots?"
Cartagena: "How Do You Mess Up Boiled Eggs?"
Chiron Review: "Would You Like to Meet Donna for Drinks?"
Coe Review: "So, What Happens Next?"
Constellations: "Why Are There Days I'm Not the Person I Want to Be?"
Free State Review: "Can You Hear Rain Over the Telephone?"
Fruita Pulp: "Who Cares About Such Things When One Has Found One's Niche in Life?" and "Have You Spoken to the Enemy?"
The Harpoon Review: "Would You Ride a Rocket into Space?"
Hawai'i Review: "Would You Like to Be on the Moon with Me, Darling, or Would You Be Afraid?"
HeartWood Literary Magazine: "What Are the Issues That Matter to You?" and "What Do You Care About?"
Heavy Feather Review: "What Has Become of Freedom?"
I-70 Review: "What Happens When You Break Down?"
The Journal of Applied Poetics: "Should I Be Animated?"
Kentucky Review: "Hello Dahling LOL Whatcha Doin?" and "What's the Point of Robbery When Nothing Is Worth Stealing?"
Little Patuxent Review: "Are You Setting Things on Fire?"
Lost Coast Review: "Do You Like Your Infamy?"
The Nassau Review: "What If the Phone Rang, and a Voice Offered You the Past?"
North Dakota Quarterly: "Just Ask the Count of Monte Cristo or Can You?"
Ocean State Review: "Getting Ready to Enjoy the Apocalypse?"
Off the Coast: "How Do I Know When I've Suffered Enough?"
Oyez Review: "Do You Think You Need a Psychiatrist?" and "Where Will the Turmoil End?"

Pacifica Literary Review: "When Will You Be Off Paper?"
Permafrost: "What Do You Often Lose?" and "What Will You Do If the Pain Subsides?"
Petrichor Review: "And Do You Also Believe That I Am So Very, Very Wicked?"
The Pikeville Review: "What's the Most Heartbreaking Thing You Can Think Of?"
Pomona Valley Review: "What Feels Better Than Noise from Our Nights?" and "Why Did You Smile?"
Quiddity: "And Indeed What Does the Price Matter, If the Trick Be Well Done?" and "So You Don't See How Very Comical Your Role Is?"
Rappahannock Review: "How Did Your Father Spend His Spare Time?"
Red Eft Review: "Is This the Noise You Hate?" and "Is It Too Late to Keep Your Secrets Safe?"
The Red Savina Review: "What Happened to Just Playing Music?"
Santa Fe Literary Review: "What If There Weren't Any Stars?"
Saranac Review: "What Is to Follow the Night That Just Ended?"
silvae magazine: "What's Your Favorite Way to Be Touched?"
Slipstream: "...What Kind of Person Am I If in Encountering Others I Love the Slimy?"
The South Carolina Review: "How Can We Distinguish What We Know from What We Believe?", "Why Are You Asking Me?", "What About You Is Original?" and "Is Forgiveness Real?"
Southern Humanities Review: "Where Is Your Troubled Faith?"
The Tishman Review: "Why Can't I Be Happy-Go-Lucky?"
Tulane Review: "Should We Be Mindful of Dreams?"
Weatherbeaten: "What Have You Shared?"
Xanadu: "Do You Think the Guitars Are Happy?"

"What If There Weren't Any Stars?" was reprinted in the anthology *Eyes Glowing at the Edge of the Woods*.

Thanks also to editors of *The Alexandria Quarterly* and *Oyez Review* for nominating "Why Do Bees Have Stripes?" and "Where Will the Turmoil End?" respectively for the Pushcart Prize.

About the Author

Ace Boggess is author of the novel *A Song Without a Melody* and three previous books of poetry: *Ultra Deep Field, The Prisoners*, and *The Beautiful Girl Whose Wish Was Not Fulfilled*. His writing has appeared *in Harvard Review, Mid-American Review, RATTLE, River Styx, North Dakota Quarterly* and many other journals. He lives in Charleston, West Virginia.

www.ingramcontent.com/pod-product-compliance
Lightning Source LLC
Chambersburg PA
CBHW070104120526
44588CB00034B/2226